The Yam Y...
& Other Veggie Carving Projects

Tom Wolfe

Text written with and photography
by Douglas Congdon-Martin

Schiffer Publishing Ltd

4880 Lower Valley Road, Atglen, PA 19310

Book Designed by Laurie A. Smucker
Typeset in Times New Roman

ISBN: 0-7643-0500-X
Printed in China

Published by Schiffer Publishing Ltd.
4880 Lower Valley Road
Atglen, PA 19310
Phone: (610) 593-1777; Fax: (610) 593-2002
E-mail: schifferbk@aol.com
Please write for a free catalog.
This book may be purchased from the publisher.
Please include $3.95 for shipping.
Try your bookstore first.

We are interested in hearing from authors
with book ideas on related subjects.

Introduction

I suppose carving vegetables is a little strange. Sure we have all carved a pumpkin or two, but the tool we use is usually a butcher knife, and the result is more than a little crude. I never thought much about carving vegetables until I got a letter from a grade school teacher asking what she could use to teach her kids to carve. Soap was too messy and wood too hard. I experimented a little before I picked up a sweet potato and began to whittle. The result was pretty good. The sweet potato was firm enough to hold a cut, but soft enough that the tools didn't need to be razor sharp to work.

But this carving isn't just for kids. It is a perfect medium to practice the use of knives and gouges. It is also a great way to develop the skills of creating character and personality in the carving.

The most fun, however, is watching the carvings as they dry. As the vegetables dry and wizen, the characters that have been carved from them develop deep lines and shapes that are totally unpredictable and totally delightful. The eyes deepen, the wrinkles multiply, and the faces take on the look of age that could not be carved.

When the pieces are totally dry, some painting provides a finishing touch.

I hope that you enjoy this new venture and that you use this book to introduce to the great and fun art of wood-carving.

The Yam Yankee

The sweet potato on the left will look like the Confederate soldier on the right after it is carved and spends a few weeks drying out. When carving the sweet potato it is important to keep your hands clean. Mold spores on the hands will find root in the sweet potato and cause it to rot.

Besides this, you can eat your shavings.

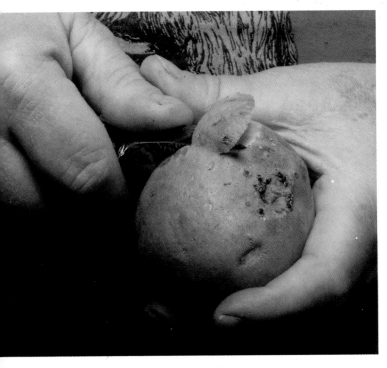

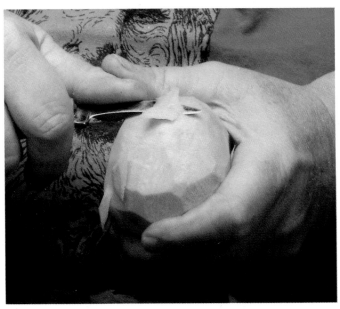

Peel the potato. This is good practice for men whose wives would like them to be more useful in the kitchen.

Even it up a little. You can take bold strokes with this medium, because it's going to shrink down anyway.

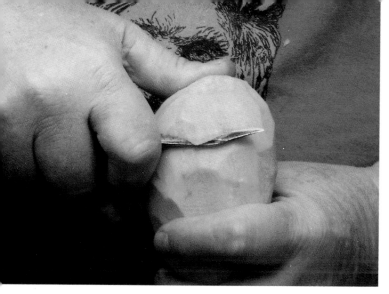

When it's all rounded up...

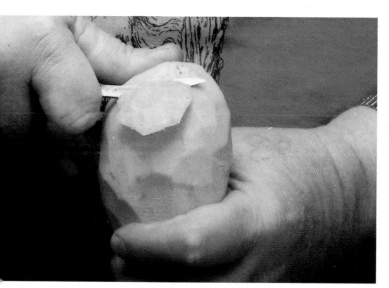

I can slice off the flat slanted top of the civil war cap.

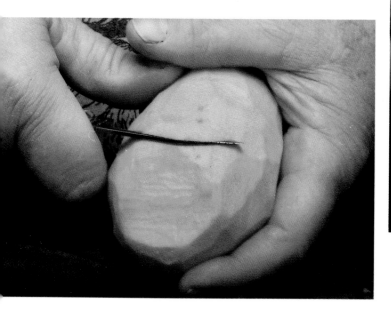

Cut down the front of the cap to the level of the brim...

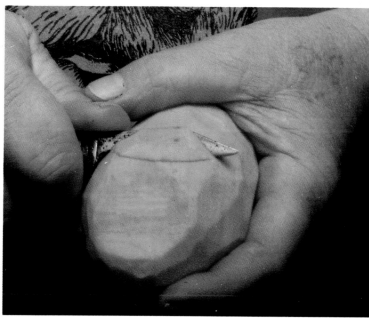

then cut in on the surface of the brim to knock out the piece.

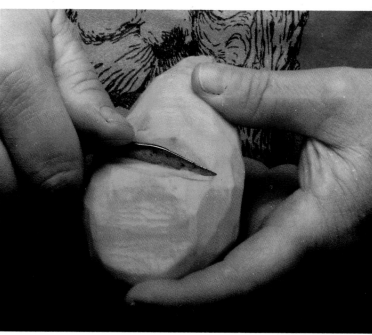

Clean up the cut.

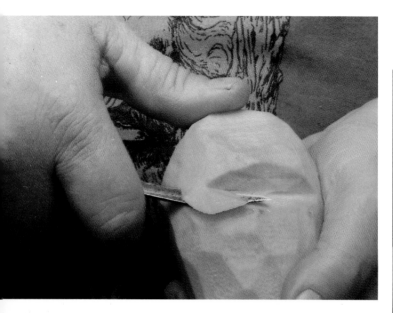

Moving to the side of the brim, carve back to the crown...

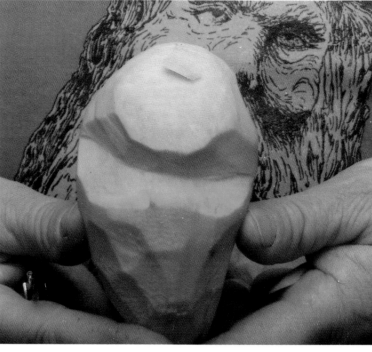

This is the result, giving you the front of the crown and the top of the hat brim.

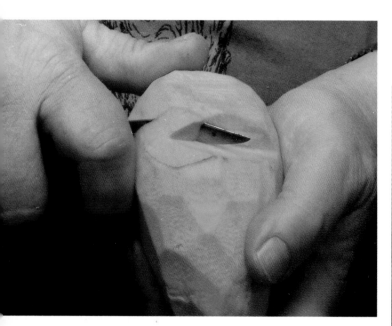

Then carve down the corner of the crown to the brim.

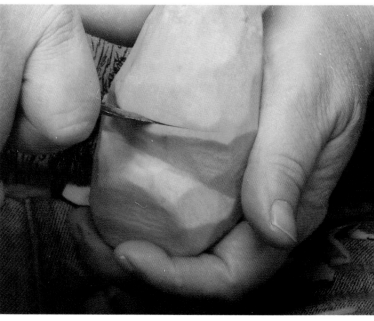

Cut across the underside of the brim, leaving about 1/8" at the edge and angled so the brim is about 1/4" thick at the forehead.

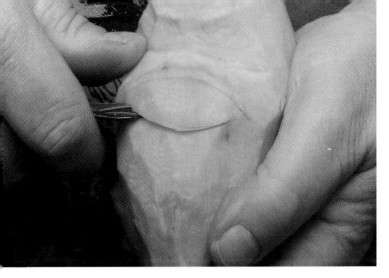

Cut back to that cut from the bridge of the nose, creating a forehead.

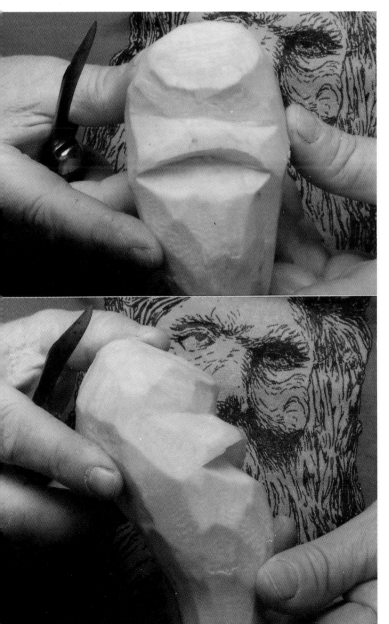

Progress from the front and the side.

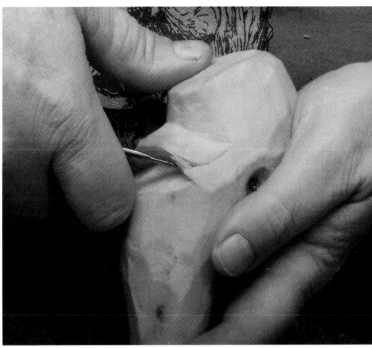

Cut the underside of the bill around the side.

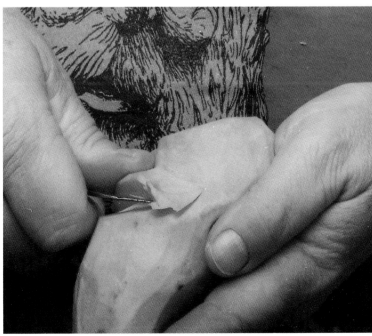

Then cut back to it from the temple. Repeat on the other side.

With a gouge, undercut the bill.

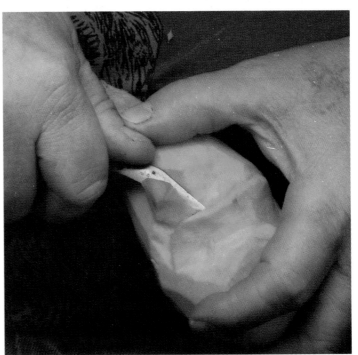

and turn the knife blade to pop it out.

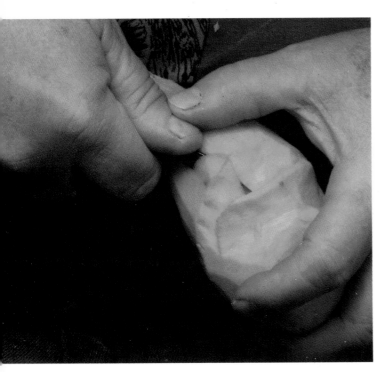

Returning to the knife, cut along the side of the nose....

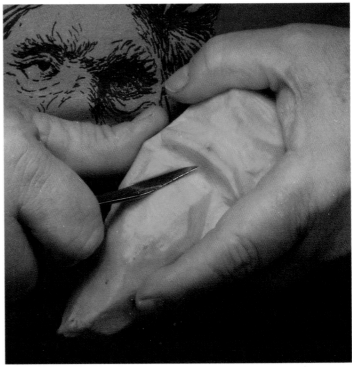

Repeat on the other side.

Cut in at the bottom of the nose...

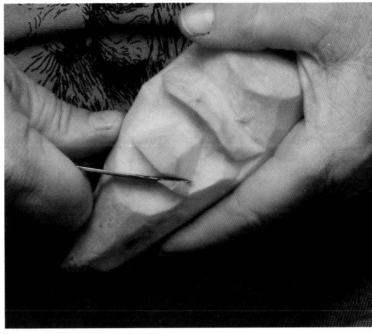

Cut the bottom corner of the nose for the nostril.

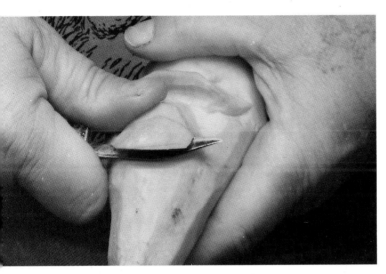

and come back to it from the surface of the moustache, popping it off when you get far enough.

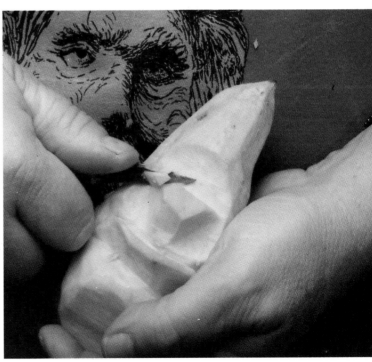

Cut back from the cheek to pop it off.

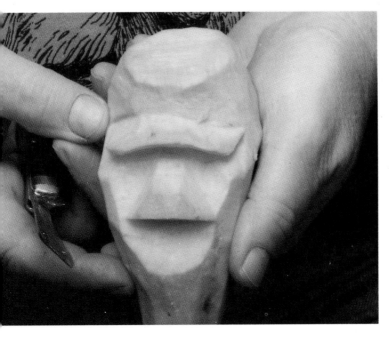

Progress. It already looks like a face.

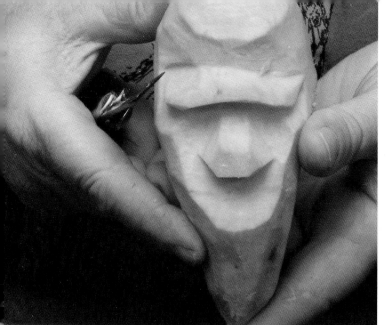

Repeat on the other side for this result.

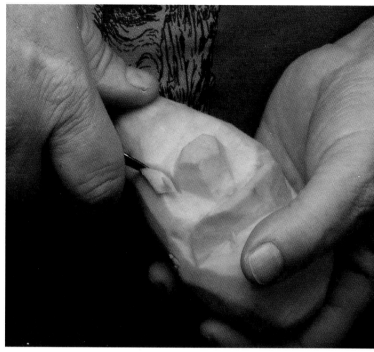

and back from the lip.

To create the smile line, cut in beside the nose...

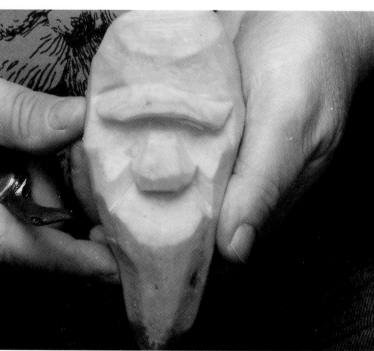

The result.

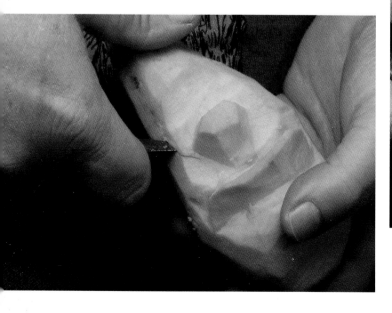

along the smile line...

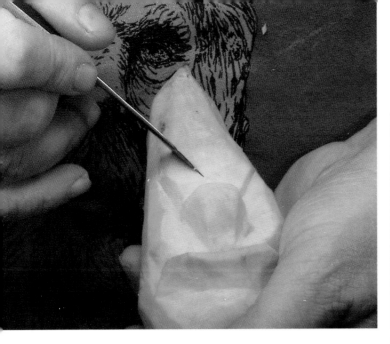

Cut along the bottom of the moustache, moving out from the center on one side...

for this result.

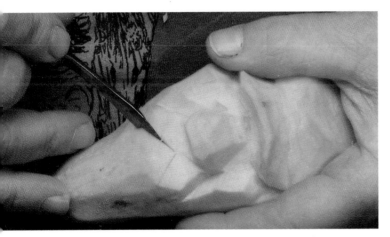

then the other.

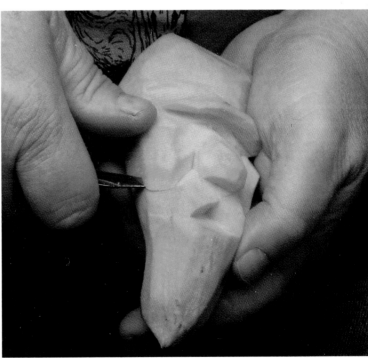

Starting at the nose, cut the top edge of the moustache. This will be a handle bar so it comes around to the side of the face.

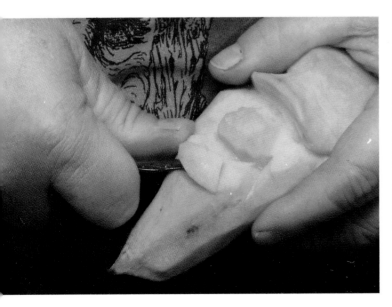

Cut back into the V formed by the moustache line from the chin...

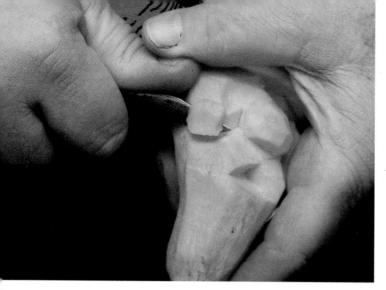

Cut back to the line from the cheek.

Progress from the front...

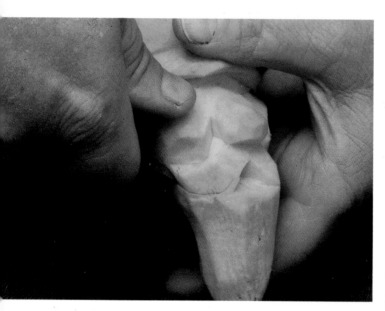

Continue the bottom line of the moustache to meet the top.

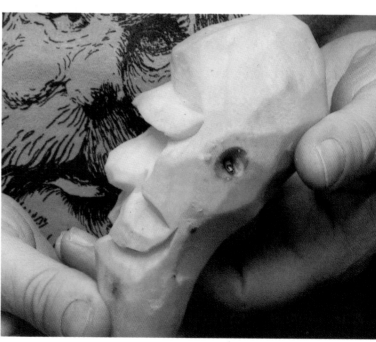

and the side.

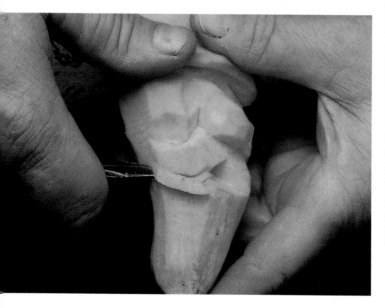

Trim back to the bottom edge from the beard.

Use a v-cut to extend the cheek line up beside the nose.

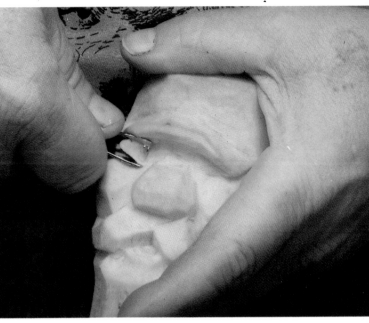

Gouge out the eyes. Be careful with the gouge. If the corner of the blade goes under the surface it is likely to break the sweet potato.

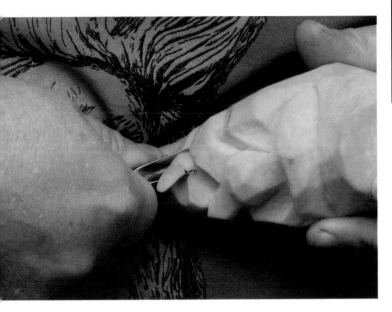

Run a gouge across the chin under the lip.

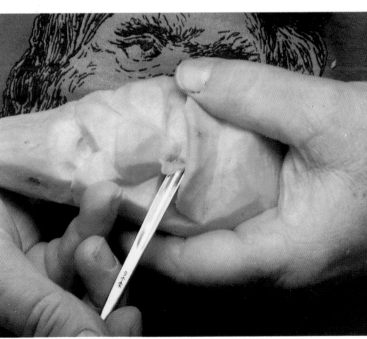

Go back with a smaller gouge and deepen the eye socket.

Clean out the mouth with same gouge, for this result.

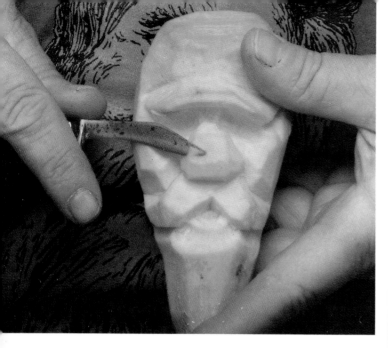

The nose is a little heavy here so I'm going to clean it up. When vegetable carvings dry, things like this become exaggerated. High points become humps and low points become valleys. Fix them now.

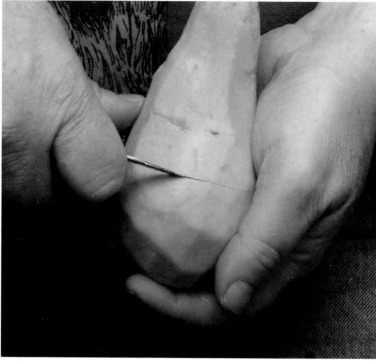

Cut a stop around the bottom of the hat in the back.

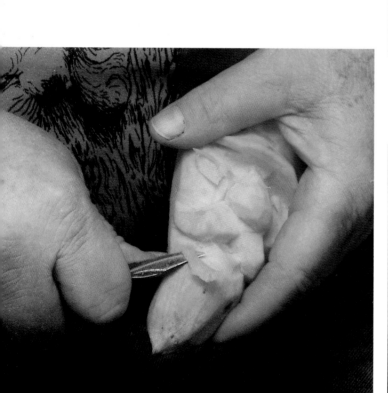

Continue to go over the piece, smoothing out the surface.

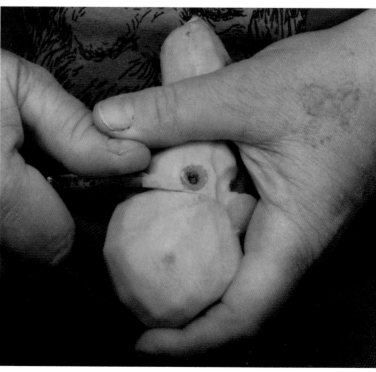

Trim back to the stop from the hair.

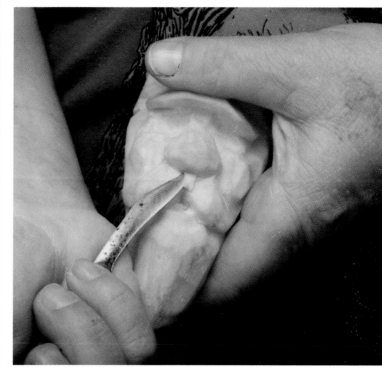

Make a v-cut to divide the two halves of the moustache.

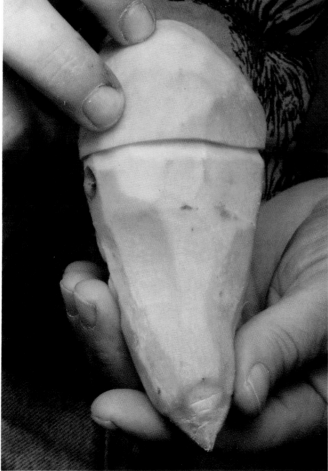

Progress.

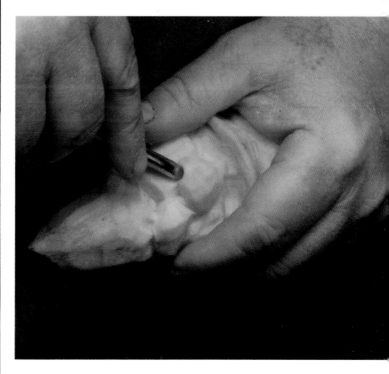

Push in a gouge to create the nostrils.

15

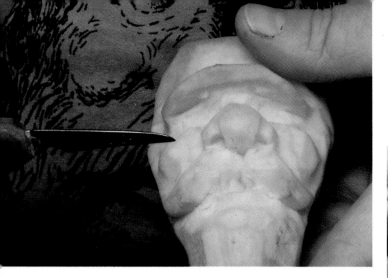

For caricature carving I like to leave the nostrils quite a bit farther apart than they naturally are.

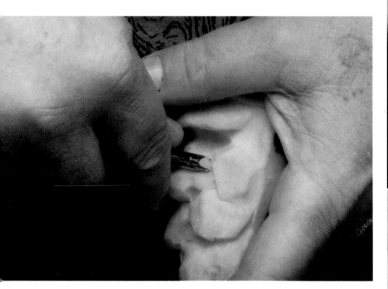

Come over the nostril flange with the gouge. It should break off easily at the smile line.

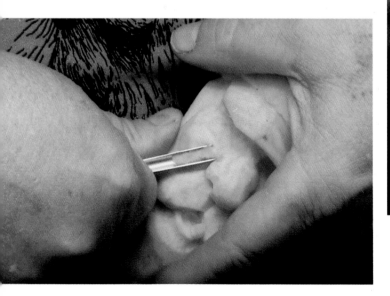

Run the gouge a little above and parallel to the cheek line to give the figure added character.

Progress.

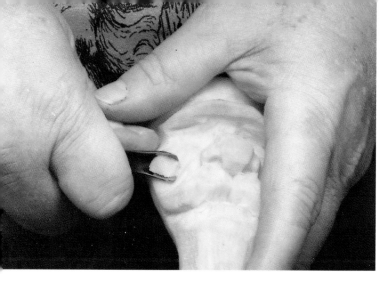

Trim and hollow the cheek a little.

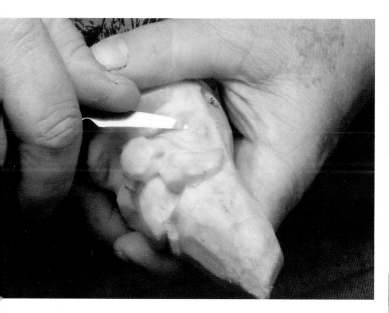

Take off the rough edges.

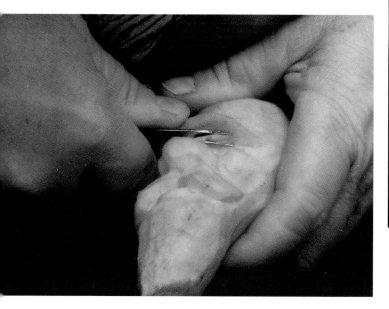

Run a v-tool across the face where the forehead meets the hat.

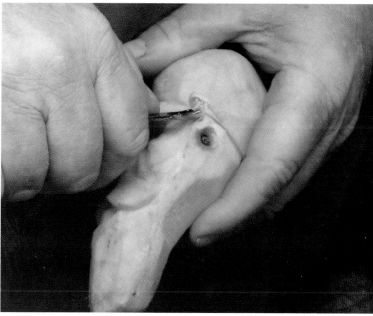

Use the v-tool to outline the major feature like the moustache and the front of the sideburn. The v-tool is better than a double knife cut for this, because the little bit left behind by the knife will be exaggerated in drying and look like something growing down in the trough.

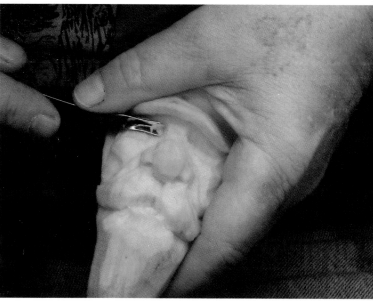

Use the v-tool to make the upper eyelid...

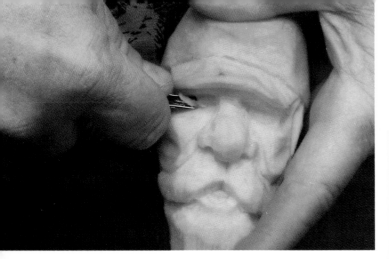

and the lower.

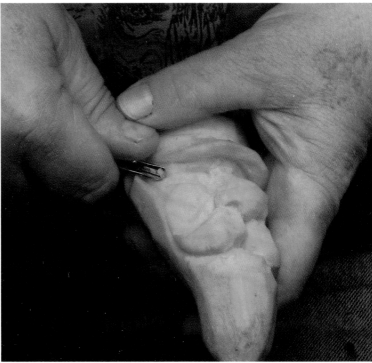

and some crow's feet at their corners.

Progress.

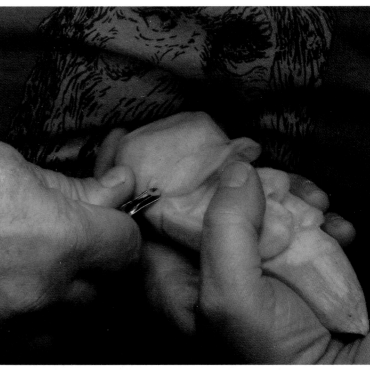

Use the v-tool to form a button for the chin strap.

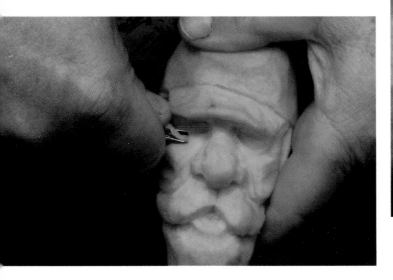

Carve the bags under the eyes...

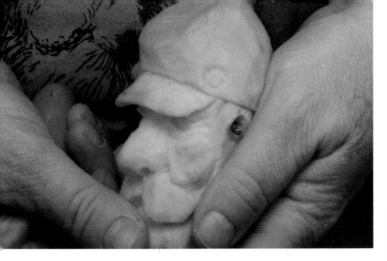

The result.

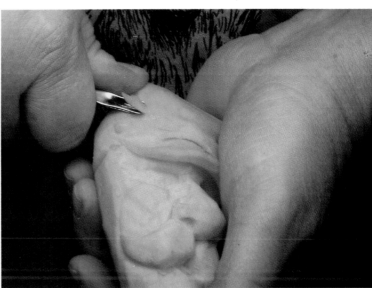

Bring a second wrinkle to join the first at the side.

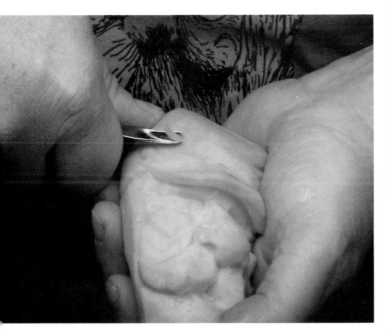

Before carving the chin strap, I'll add the wrinkles to the front of the hat. Make the start of the top edge of the strap.

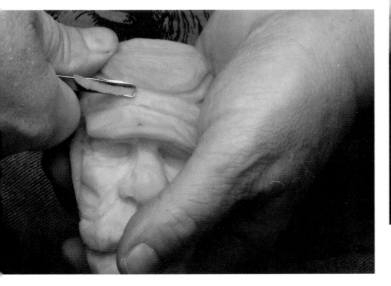

Then go under the top of the hat and form a wrinkle

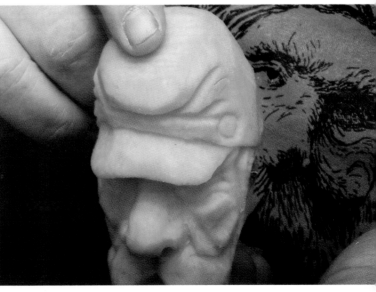

The result.

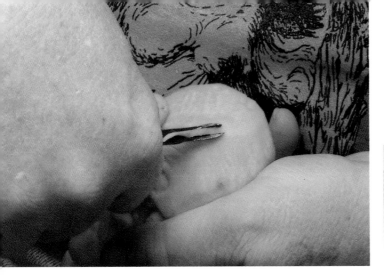

Go around the flat part of the cap outside...

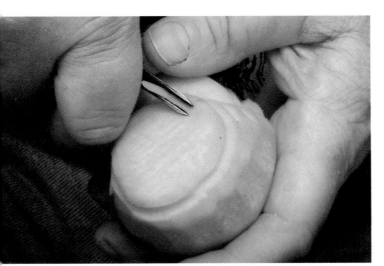

and inside.

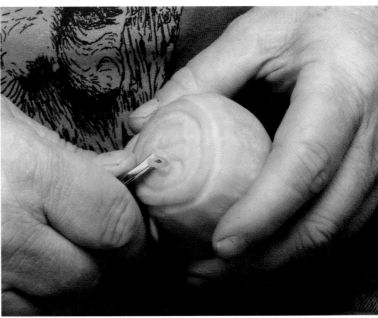

I've chosen to carve a U.S. in the flat surface of the cap.

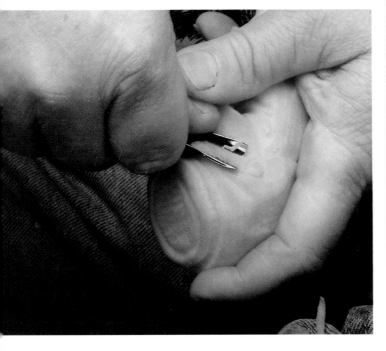

A flatter gouge gives a little cup shape to the surface of the chin strap.

I want to give a cupped appearance to the brim, without making it too thin. A flatter gouge should do the job.

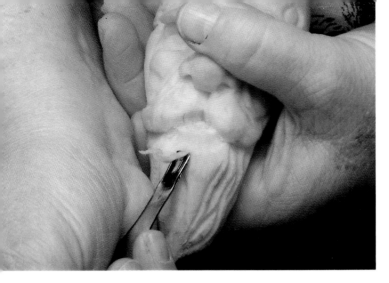

Use the v-tool to add hairlines in the beard and the moustache. The hairs should follow the line of the handlebars.

A chopstick or a dowel goes into the hole to support the figure while it dries.

Cut a groove in the back.

Look the piece over to see what it needs. On this piece I need to carry the hatband around the back of the cap.

With a narrow gouge, make a hole in the base of the head.

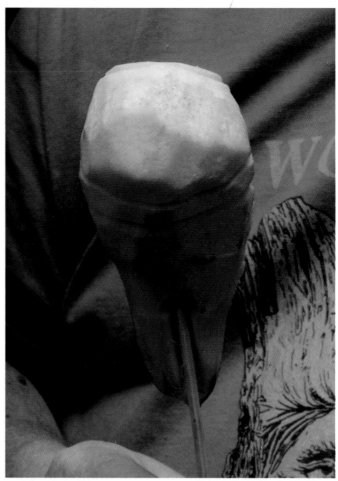

Ready to dry.

The Homegrown Gnome

The gnome in this sweet potato is crying to get out.

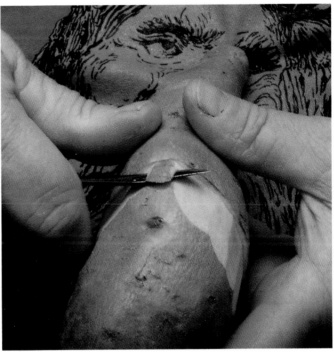

Trim back to the cap from the head.

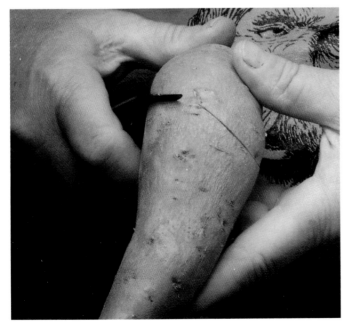

Cut around the brim of the hat.

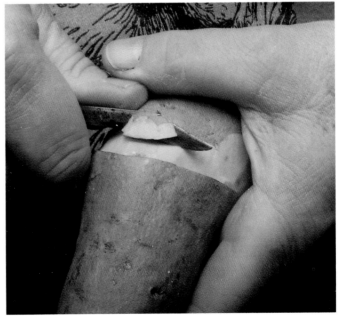

Cut out the bridge of the nose, up to the brow.

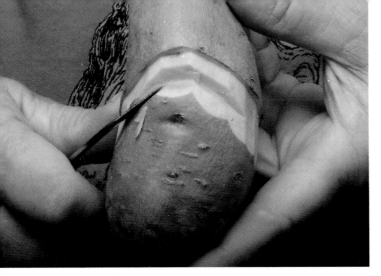

Carry the brow around to each side.

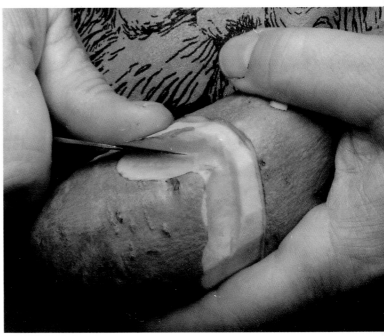

Carve down on each side of the nose.

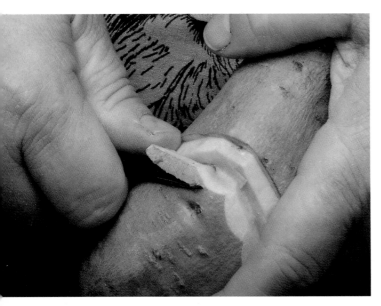

Gouge out for the eyes...

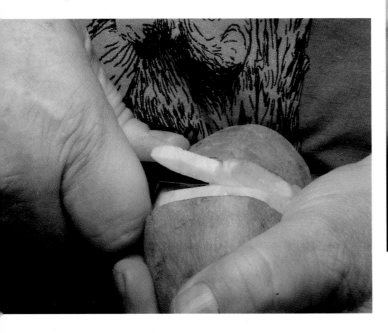

on both sides, cutting back to the bridge of the nose.

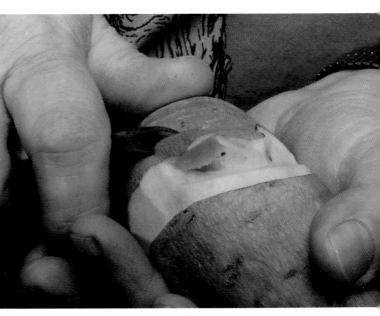

A turn of the knife will usually break away the waste.

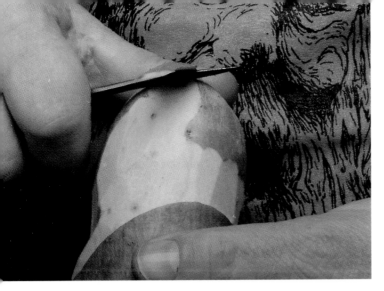

Clean up the rest of the head below the hat.

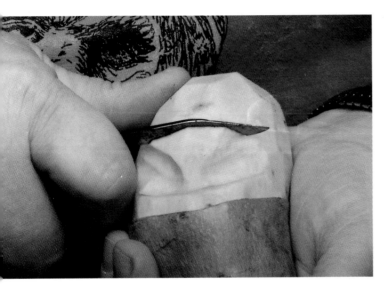

Cut into the bottom of the nose...

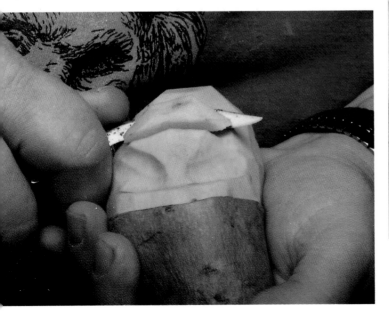

and back to it from the lip. I'm going for a kind of wide nose.

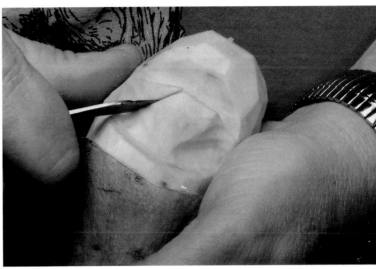

Knock off the lower corners of the nose for the nostrils by cutting in...

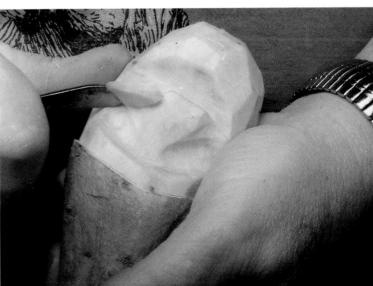

and back across from the cheek.

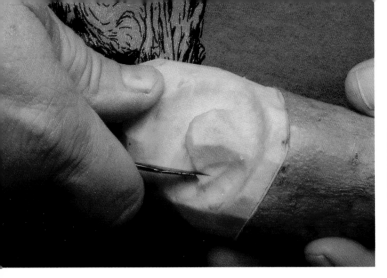

Create the smile line. First cut in along side the nose.

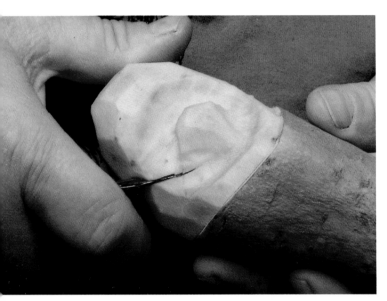

Then cut down along the cheek...

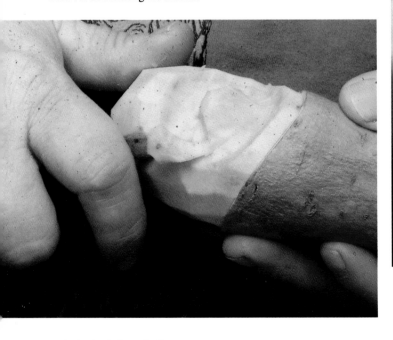

and trim back from the lip.

Progress.

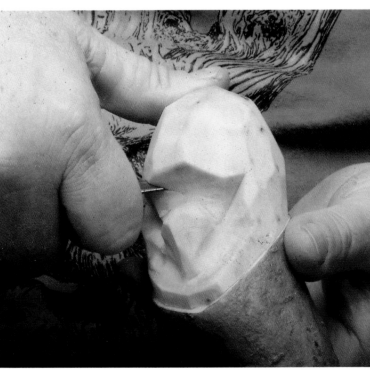

The mouth area is created the same way. A cut along the top lip one way...

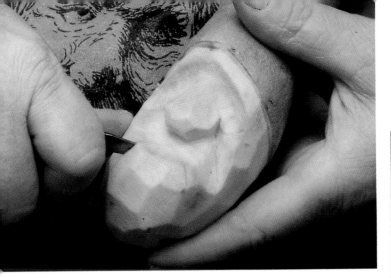

and the other.

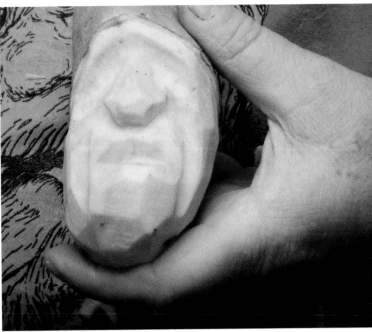

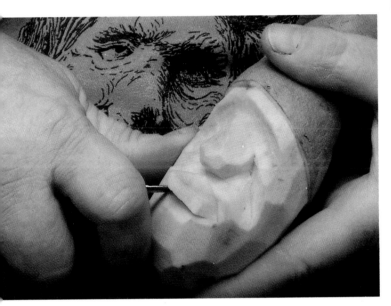

This is followed by a flat cut along the lower lip.

The result.

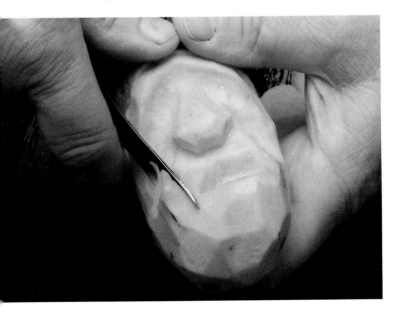

This figure will not have a moustache. To create the mouth, run a gouge down either side of the mouth, into the chin.

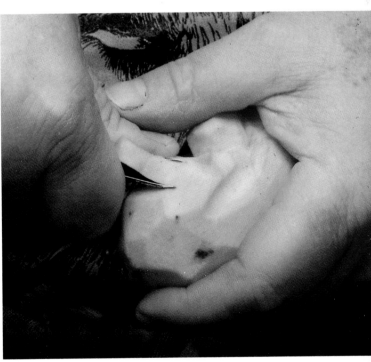

With the same gouge go across the chin under the lower lip.

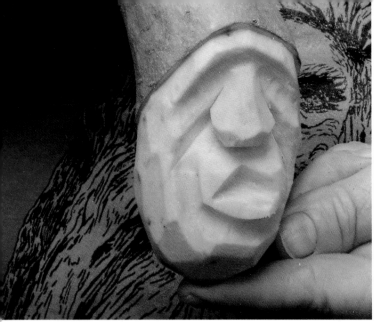

The result.

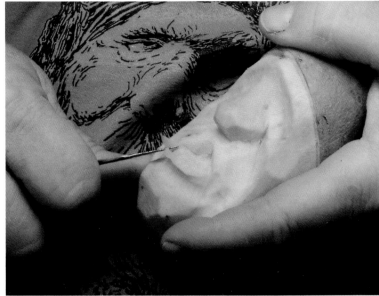

Smooth the lower lip.

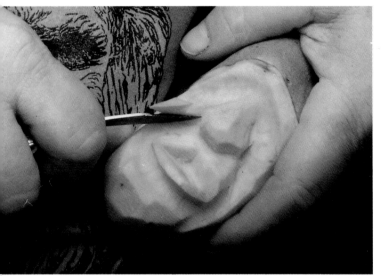

Shape the upper lip.

Bring out the chin by coming up one side of the chin and under the bottom lip.

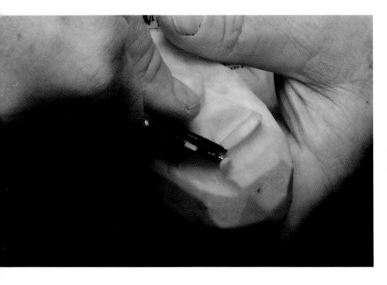

The lower lip should appear to go under the upper lip at the corner. This is done by clipping off the ends of the lower lip with a gouge.

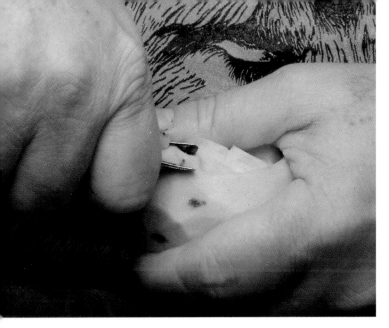

Go underneath the chin and back up the other side.

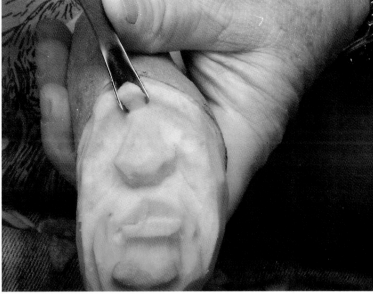

Create a separation between the eyebrows.

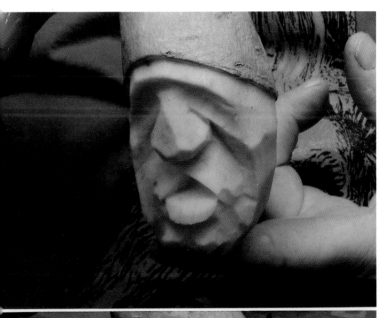

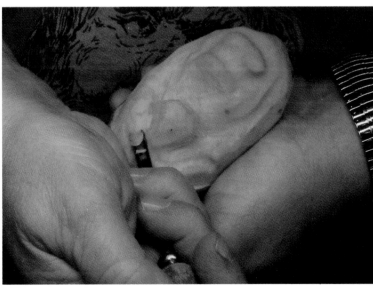

Deepen the eye sockets.

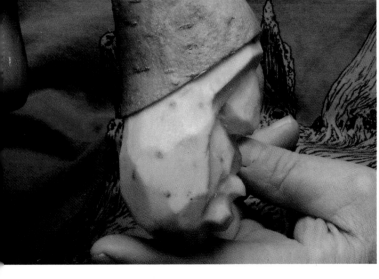

Progress

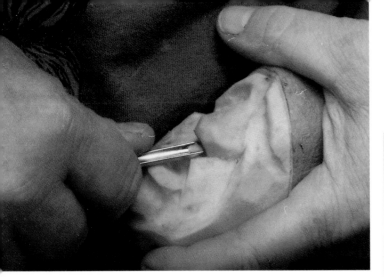

Add the philtrum.

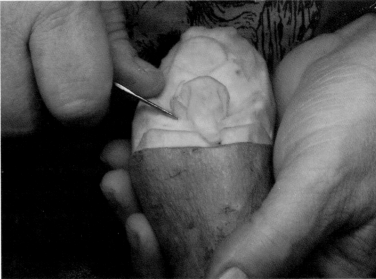

and clean up around it with a knife.

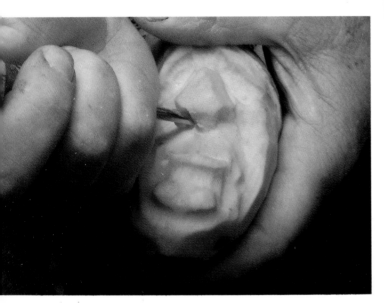

The nostrils are carved with the cup side of the gouge away from the nose.

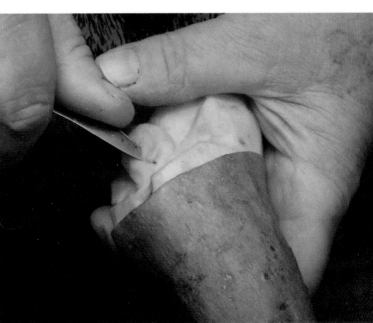

Any undercuts need to be cleaned up or they will cause uneven drying.

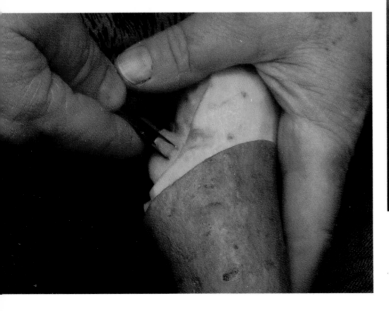

Come over the top of the nostril with the gouge...

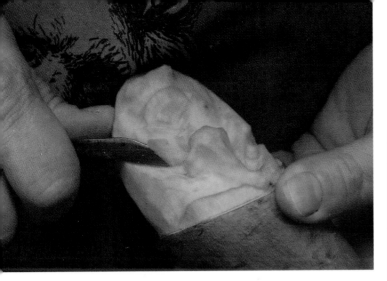

I want to add a little curl back from the lip.

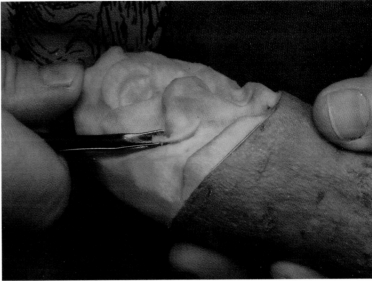

Add a few character lines parallel to the smile lines.

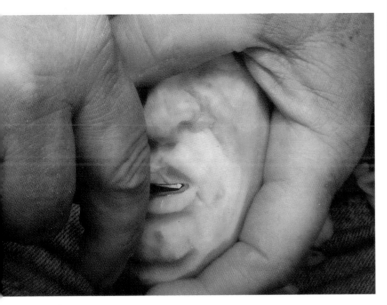

Use the gouge to add a little bit of a tongue.

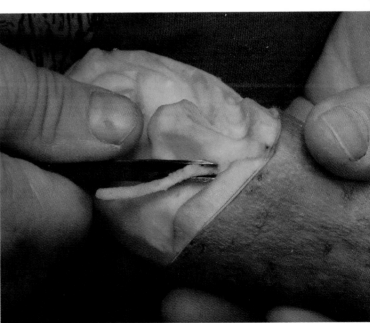

This one runs right up into the corner of the eye.

The gouge creates the cup of the center of the tongue.

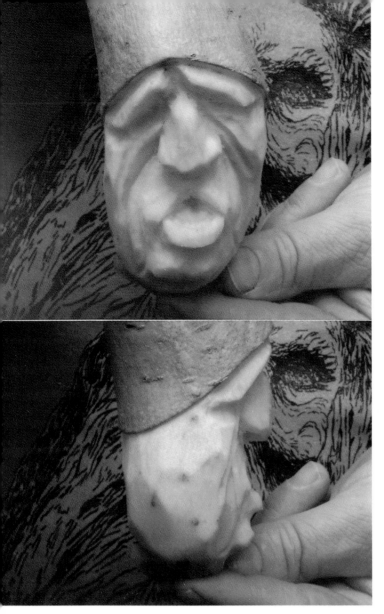

Progress.

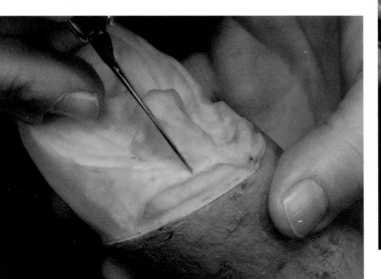

The eyes are made by cutting triangles at the corners. At the inside corner cut along the upper lid...

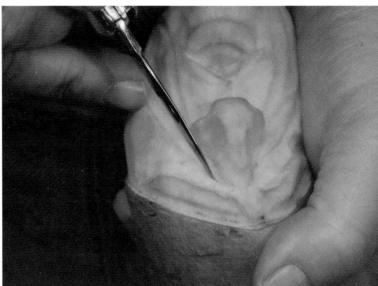

along the lower lid...

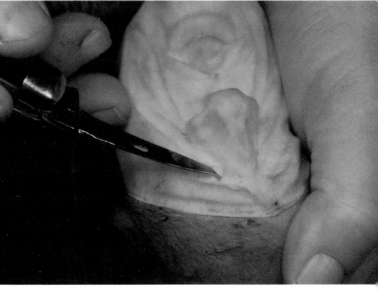

and back into it from the surface of the eye, lifting out the nitch.

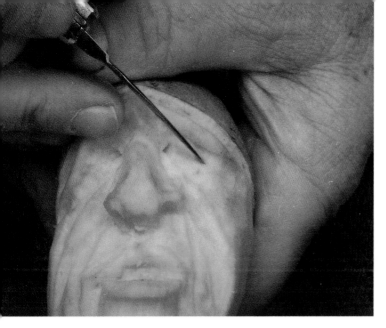

Cut along the upper lid...

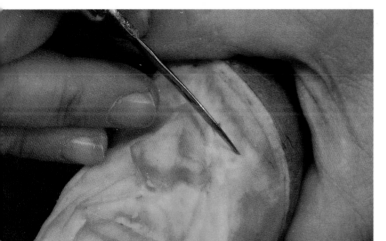

the lower lid....

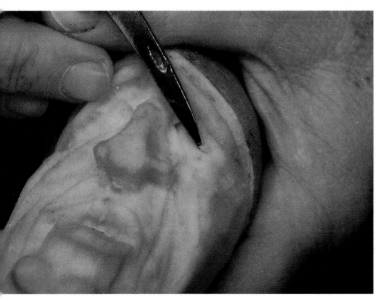

and back into the outer corner from the surface of the eye.

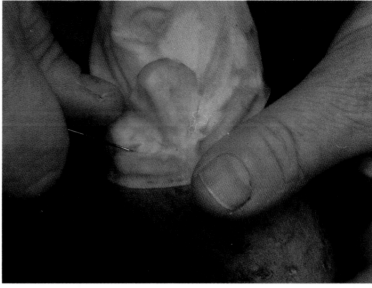

Connect the triangles with a stop at the top of the eye....

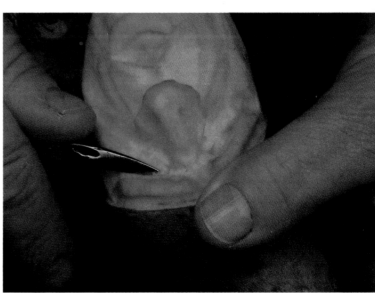

and shave back to the stop from the eyeball.

Do the same at the bottom of the eye...a stop...

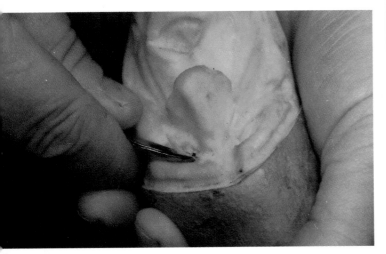

followed by a shave.

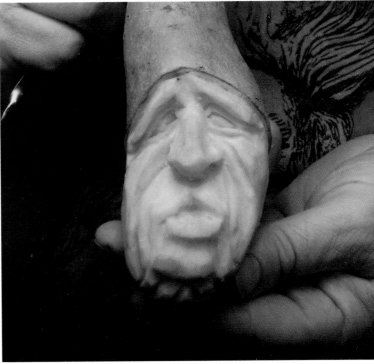

Progress. The waddles under the chin add some age.

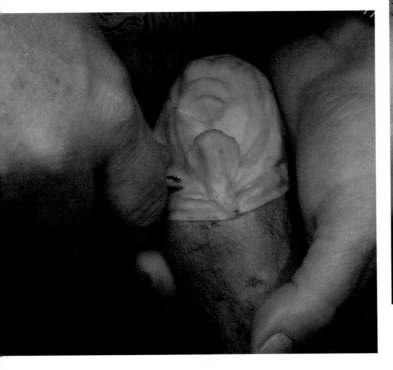

A v-tool is used to create the eyebrow and the bag under the eye.

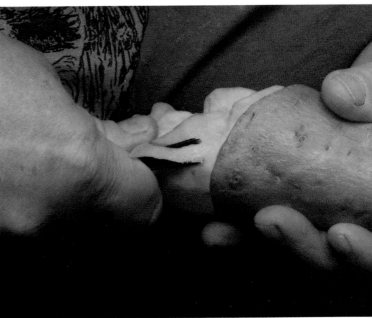

Create some sideburn lines. The ears are under the hat.

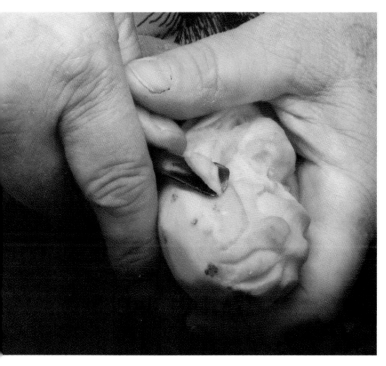

A notch out of the cheek adds character.

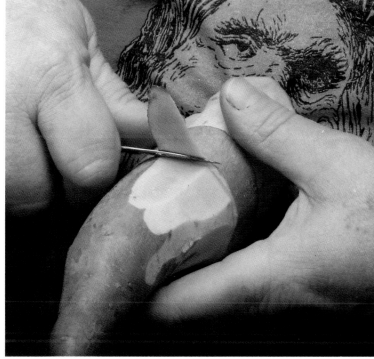

Clean back to it. The skin will add some variety of the texture. Leaving it on the whole hat would impair proper drying.

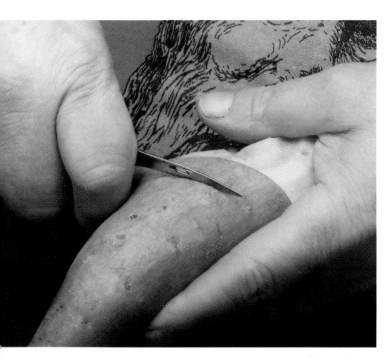

Run a line slightly above the bottom of the cap.

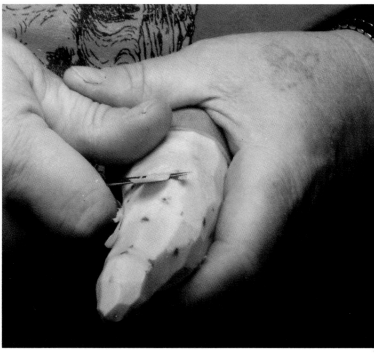

Go over the figure with a knife to clean it up.

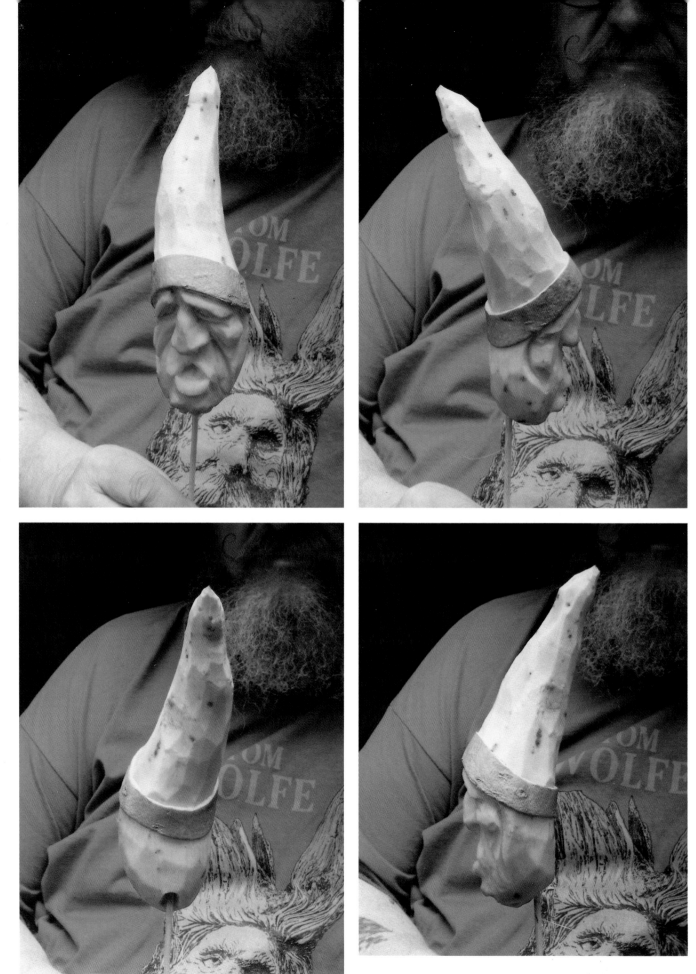

Ready to dry.

Wild Wolfe's Wizened Wizard

This large sweet potato will make a great wizard.

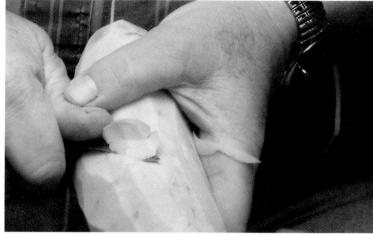

Use a scooping cut to create the eye sockets...

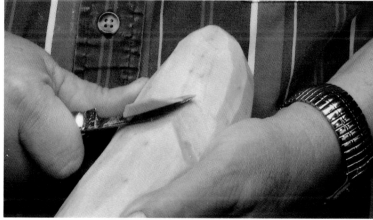

on both sides.

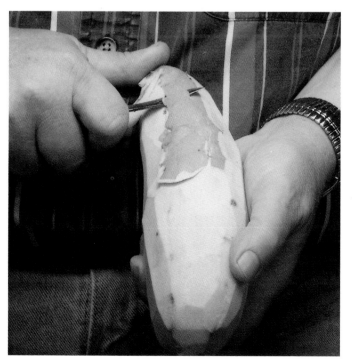

Peel the potato completely.

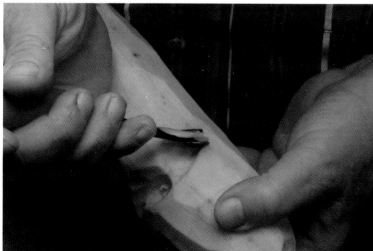

Use a gouge to deepen the socket and carry it into the temple.

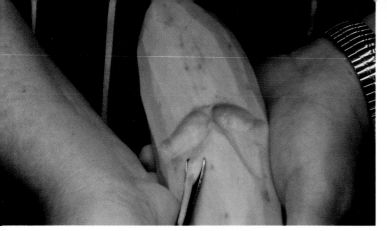

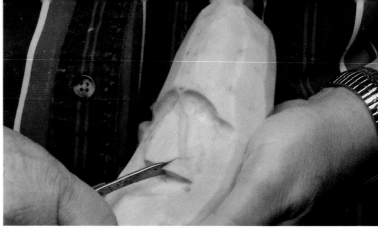

Next come up beside the nose with the gouge.

Knock off the lower corners of the nose, cutting straight in....

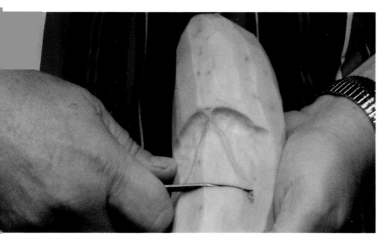

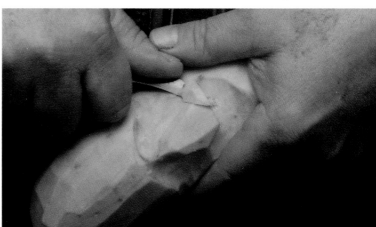

Cut in at the bottom of the nose...

then back from the cheek.

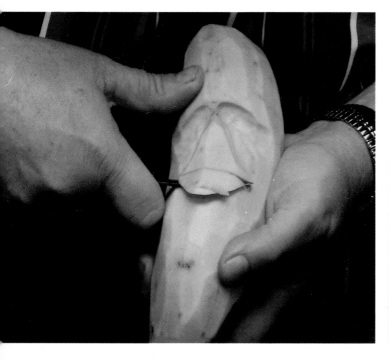

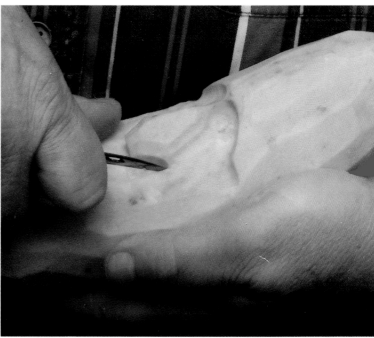

and up from the upper lip.

Create the start of the smile line by cutting in at the back of the nostril...

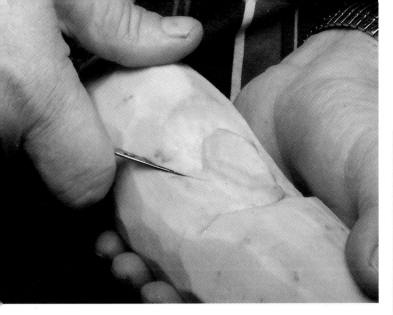

down along the smile line...

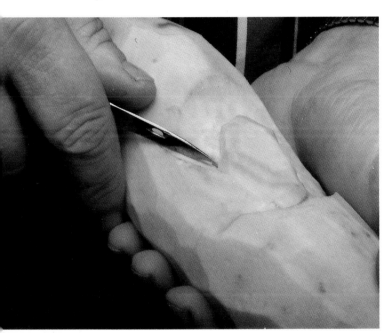

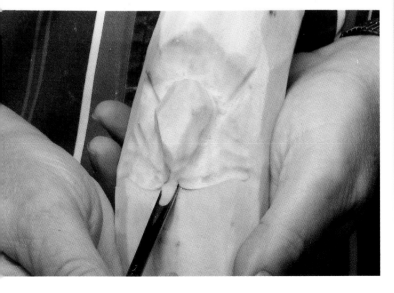

Separate the eyebrows.

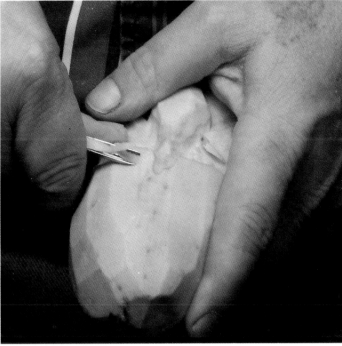

Cut a groove above the eyebrow with the gouge.

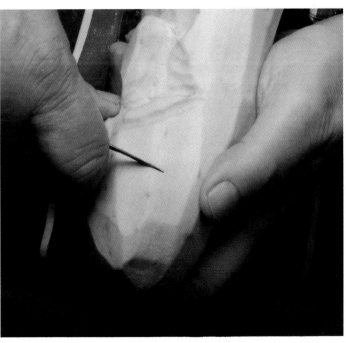

The part of the hair is made with three cuts. This one...

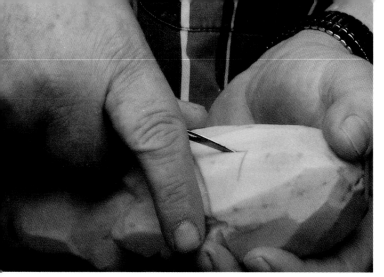

one perpendicular to it....

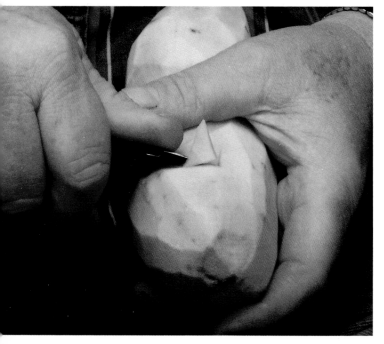

and a third along the surface of the forehead to clean it out.

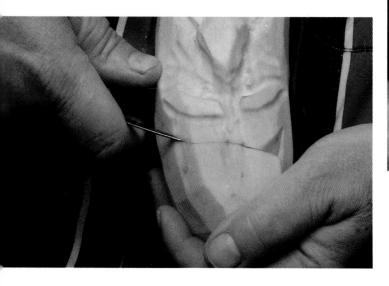

Continue the hairline across the forehead.

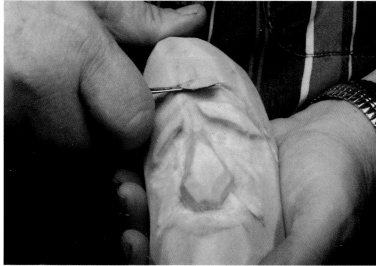

Trim back to it.

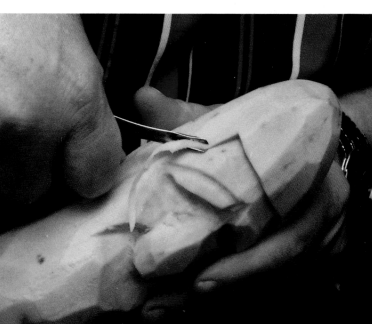

Switching to a v-tool, I bring the hairline up the side of the face.

The result.

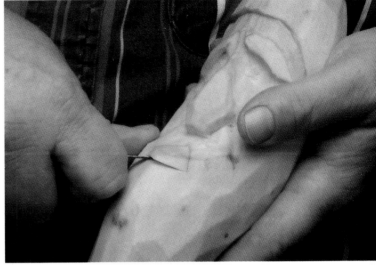

three.

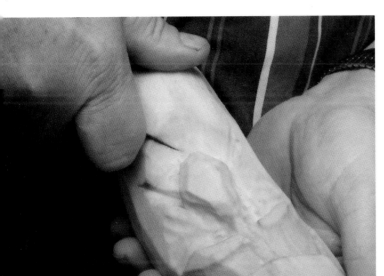

As before we make the mouth with three cuts. One...

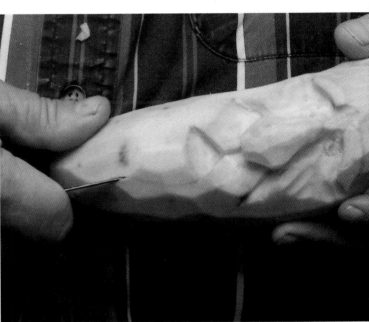

Carry the moustache line down into the beard.

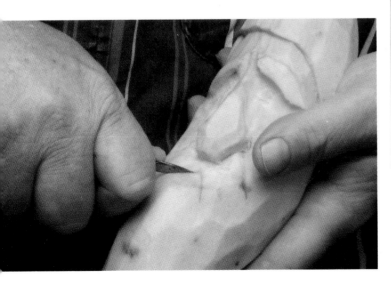

two...

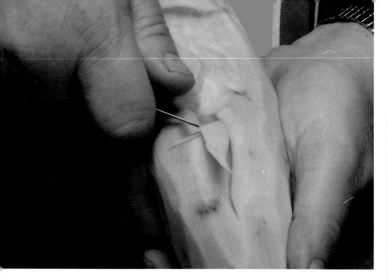

Trim back to it from the inside.

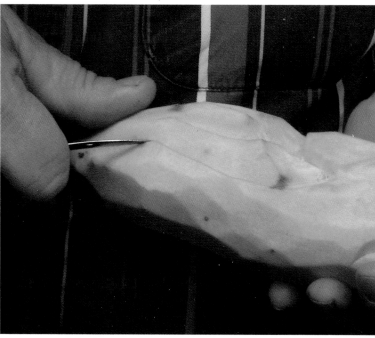

Cut the outside line of the moustache...

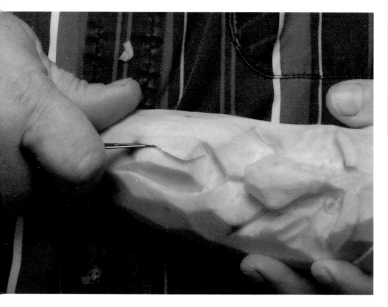

Do the same on the other side.

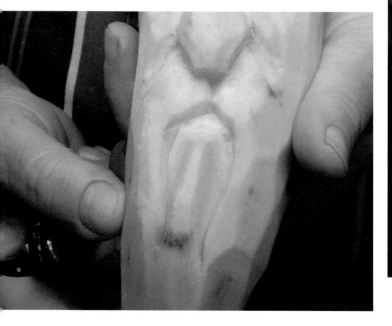

Progress.

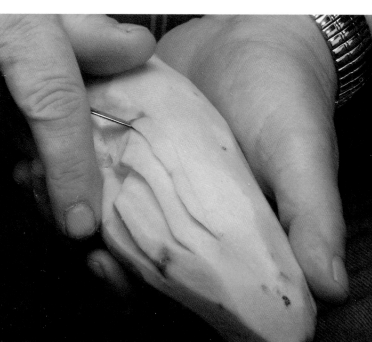

and trim back to it from the moustache.

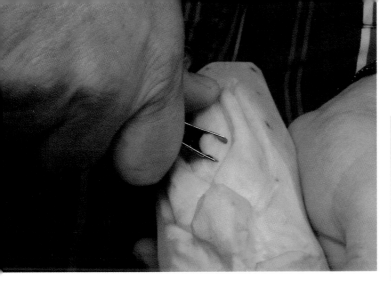

Gouge under the lower lip.

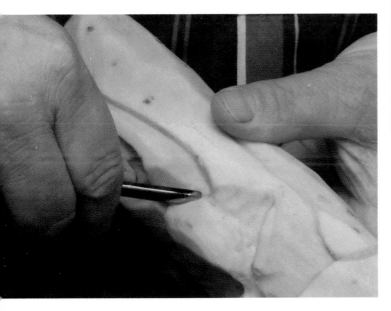

Gouge the nostrils, breaking the cut off at the face.

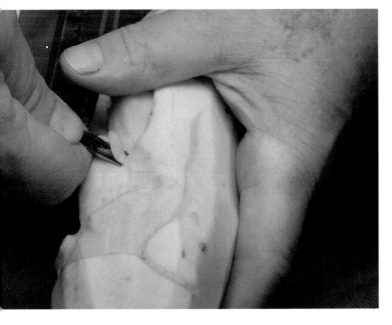

Gouge over the nostril flange.

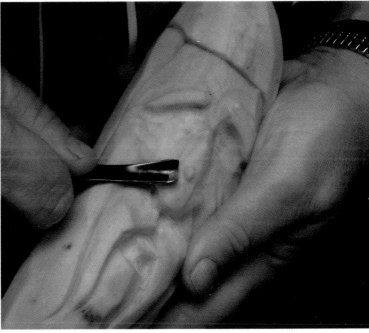

Blend the groove into the nose and clean up the surface.

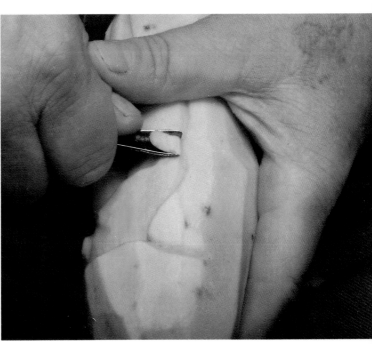

Use the gouge to shape the temple and the upper line of the cheek.

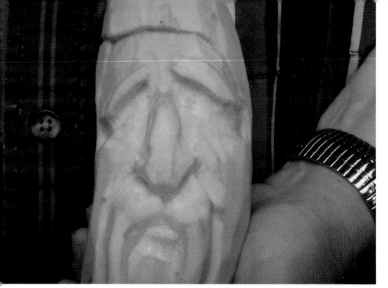

Progress.

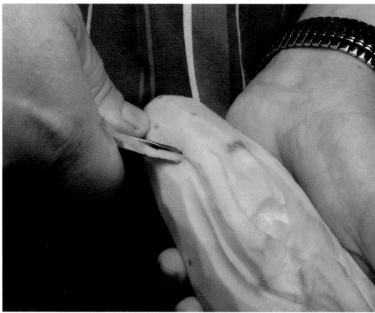

Add some curly lines to the beard using the v-tool.

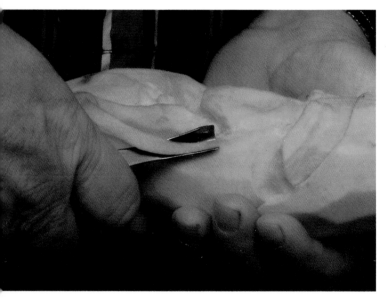

Add some character lines, like this one that parallels the smile line and runs into the beard.

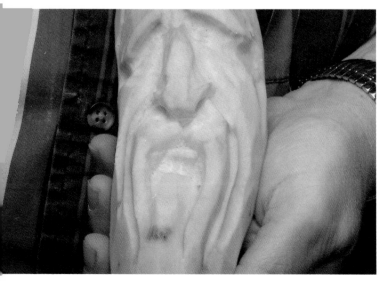

The result.

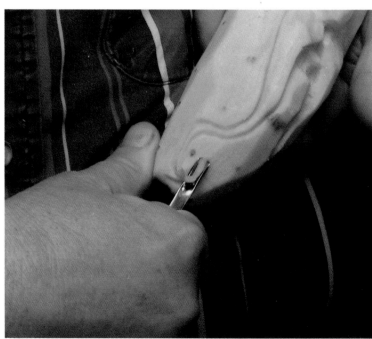

Add some hairs to the beard. Notice that I've lapped the end of this cut with the previous one. That adds some realism to the hair, and I always try to do this.

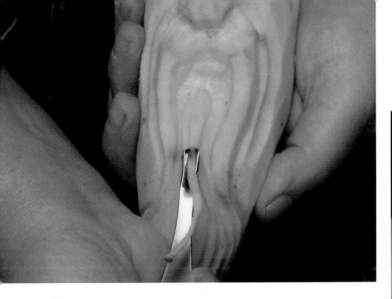

There is nothing worse than straight hair lines, so keep it moving.

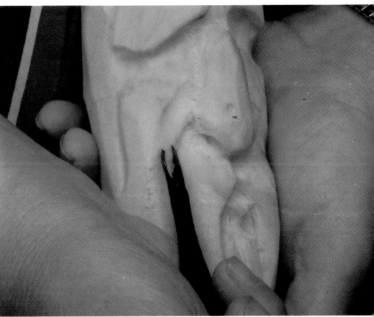

Here I am coming up with a veiner, starting with a curved hairline...

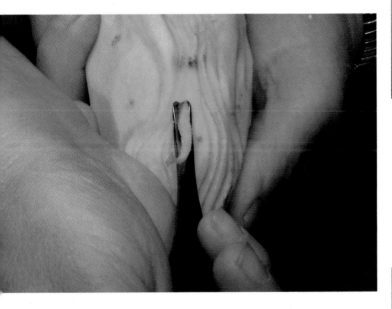

You can fade a line out by running into another, but you don't want to cross lines. That gives a crosshatch that doesn't look right, except on a fish's back.

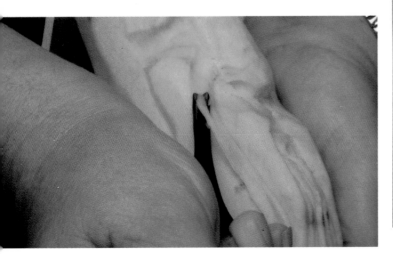

Carry a hairline into the character line you created earlier, tapering the cut so it ends before it gets to the face.

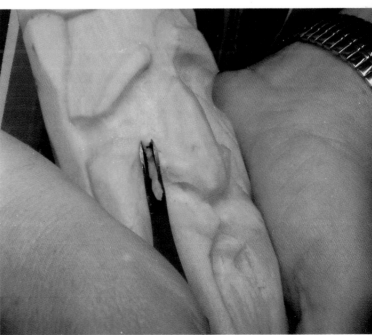

then straightening up so it becomes a line in the face.

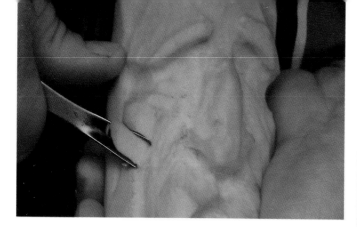

With a flatter gouge create the hollow of the cheek, carrying it to the beard.

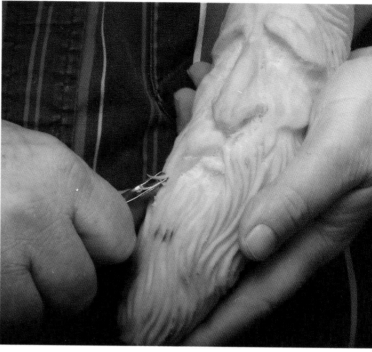

The hairs of the moustache should flow from the center of the lip.

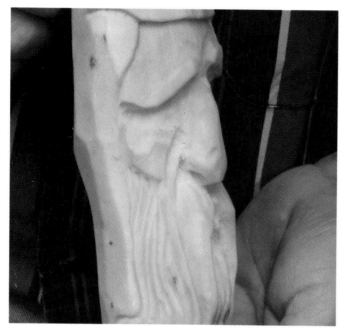

Round off the cheek for this result.

Continue the hair at the top of the head.

Don't forget the eyebrows.

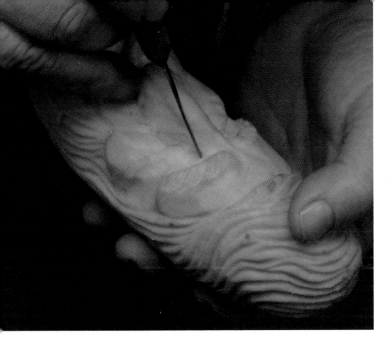

The eyes are elongated triangles. Cut a short side at the nose.

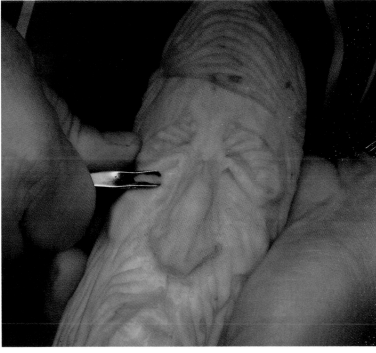

Add some wrinkles around the eyes.

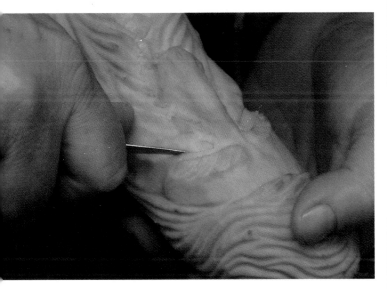

the top line out to the corner...

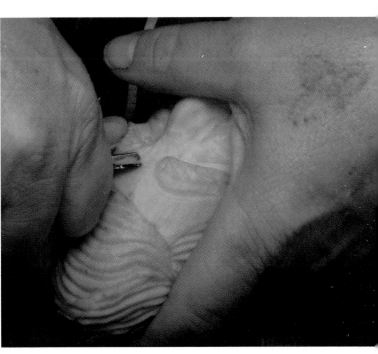

Add some wrinkles to the forehead.

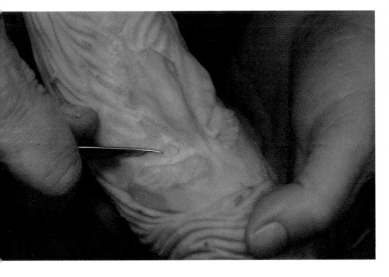

and the bottom side cut to lift out the triangle.

Finished.

The Gallery

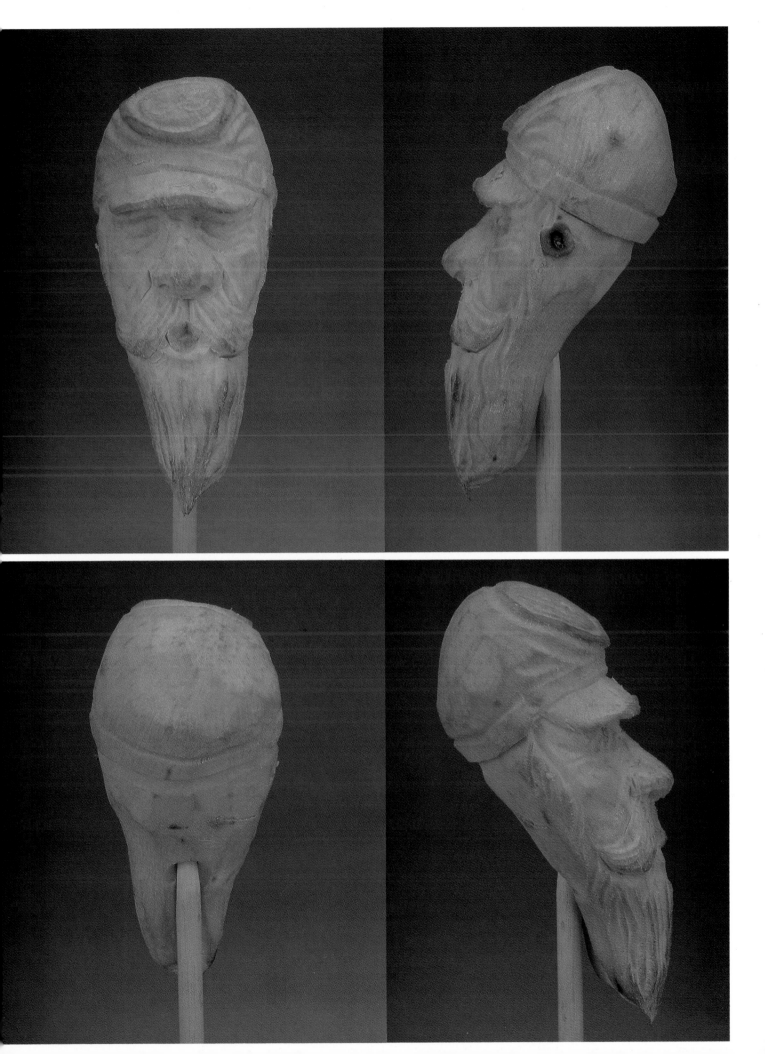

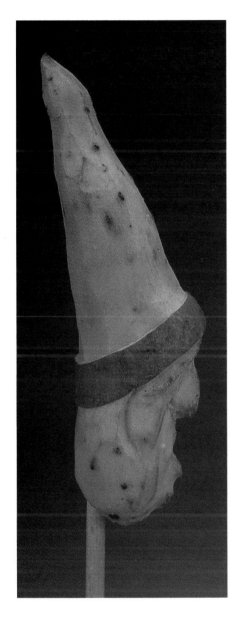

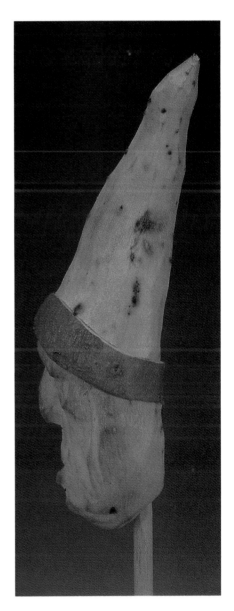

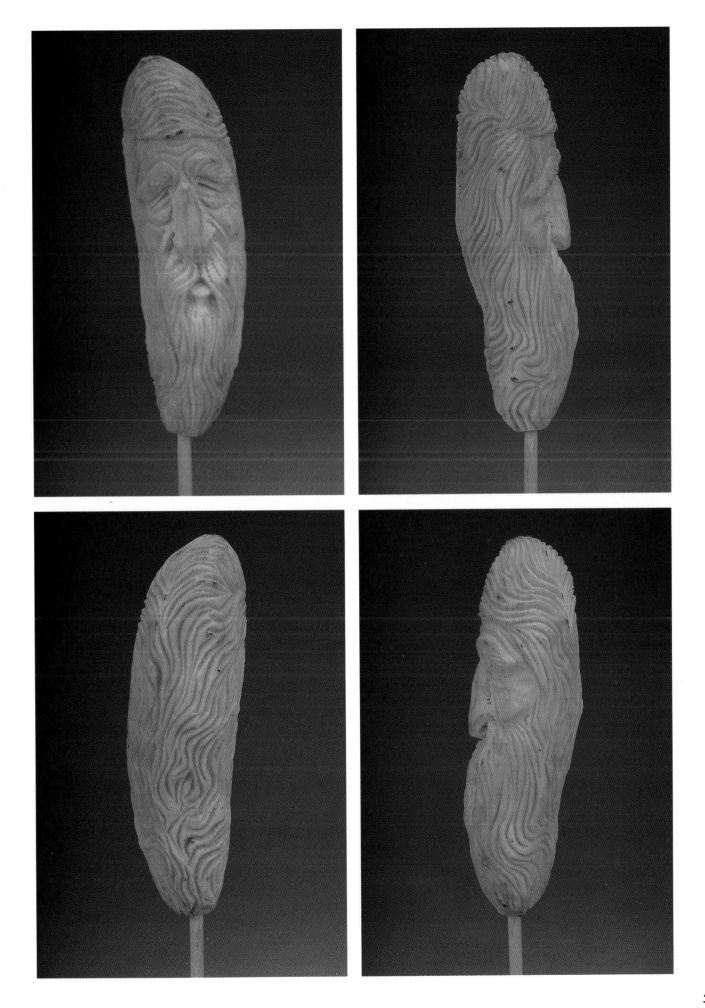

55

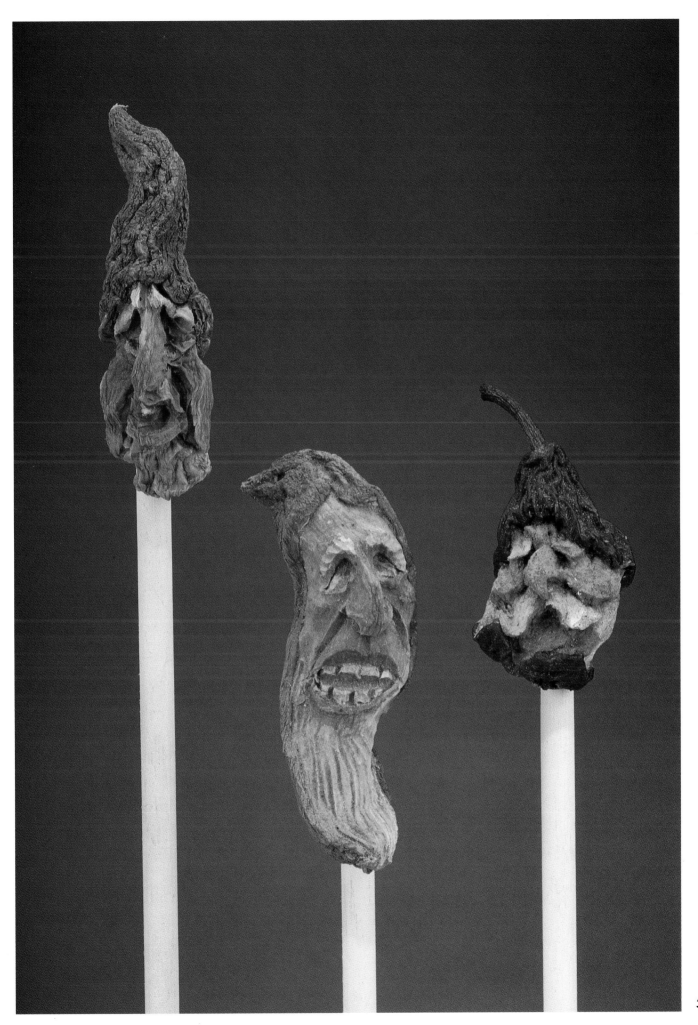

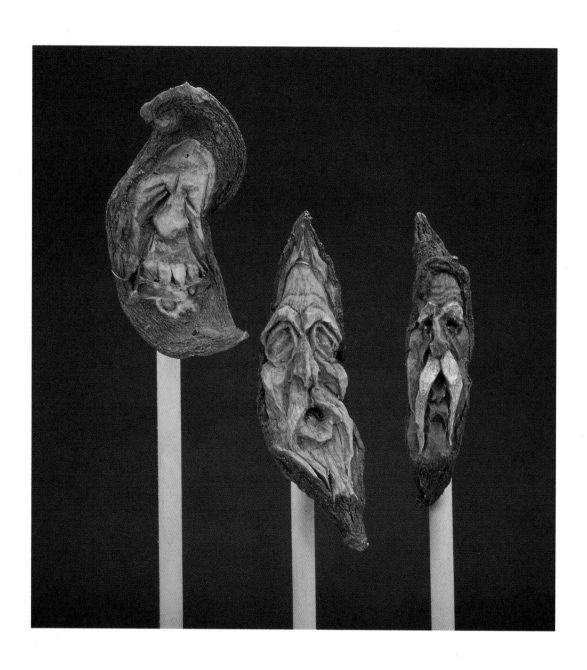